Belongs To:

Made in the USA
Monee, IL
11 March 2021

62495086R00066